Empathy in Action
Transforming Communication through Emotional Intelligence

Table of Contents

Chapter 1. Introduction

Get ready to embark on an invigorating journey where mind meets heart; shifting paradigms, breaking barriers and reshaping the communication landscape. Our Special Report, "Empathy in Action: Transforming Communication through Emotional Intelligence" is not just full of insights, but it is a key that unlocks the door to a world where communication is more fruitful, and relationships are more fulfilling. Imbued with case studies, expert opinions, and practical ways to hone your emotional intelligence, this report will inspire you to purchase it as an investment in turning every interaction into an opportunity to connect. Stand on the shoulders of giants who have travelled the path and see the transformation empathy brings into your personal and professional life! The future of communication starts now, and it starts with you. Let's dive into the heart of empathy!

Chapter 2. Unlocking the Power of Empathy

Empathy is the capacity to understand or feel what another person is experiencing from within their frame of reference. It's akin to standing in someone else's shoes and viewing the world through their eyes. This chapter strives to present a deep understanding of the power of empathy in the realm of communication.

2.1. The Concept of Empathy

Empathy at a fundamental level is the ability to understand and share the feelings of others. Yet, to truly grasp its power, we must delve into the intricate aspects of empathy. From a psychological perspective, empathy encompasses two principal components: cognitive and emotional.

Cognitive empathy refers to our capacity to comprehend another's perspective or mental state. Meanwhile, emotional empathy refers to our capacity to respond with an appropriate emotion to another's mental state. An ideal empathetic response involves a combination of both.

In the realm of communication, empathetic individuals can 'feel' what their communication partners are feeling. They can perceive emotions, thoughts, and attitudes, enhancing the depth and quality of existing connections and paving the way for robust new ones.

2.2. Empathy and Emotional Intelligence

Empathy is also a central component of emotional intelligence, an ability crucial for effective communication. Emotional intelligence, as defined by psychologists John D. Mayer and Peter Salovey, involves the ability to identify, comprehend, and manage emotions. And so, empathy, through its connection to emotional intelligence, forms a necessity for effective communication.

The emotional intelligence model proposed by Daniel Goleman posits five components: self-awareness, self-regulation, internal motivation, empathy, and social skills. Among these, empathy stands as a vital part, positioning us to understand others better and respond appropriately to their emotional states.

2.3. Empathy in Communication

Comprehending the cognitive and emotional aspects of empathy can radically transform our communication style. Focusing on empathetic communication means paying attention to the other person's perspective during each interaction. It means genuinely listening and allowing the other person's emotional state to inform our responses.

But how does empathy play out in practical, everyday communication? Considered one of the active listening techniques, Empathic Listening, is an excellent example. It involves understanding the speaker's feelings and meanings from their perspective and conveying that understanding back to the speaker. Empathic listening fosters deeper relationships, ensuring the other party feels truly heard and understood.

2.4. Case Study: X-Company and the Power of Empathy

Consider X-Company, a multinational corporation that realized the true power of empathy in reshaping its communication. The company's management noticed a drop in engagement levels amongst its staff, leading it to revamp its internal communication strategy. The shift involved promoting empathy at the core of its communication.

Employee training programs on empathetic communication were introduced, special attention was given to encourage active listening, and feedback mechanisms were implemented company-wide. Over time, X-Company started witnessing a significant improvement in the quality of interactions, leading to stronger relationships, increased team cohesion, and improved employee morale.

2.5. Harnessing Empathy in Personal and Workplace Communication

Harnessing the power of empathy in our personal and professional lives involves more than endorsing it theoretically. It demands continuous practice, encompassing self-awareness, active listening, and a sincere desire to understand others.

In the personal sphere, empathetic communication could mean listening to a friend's troubles without rushing to give advice, acknowledging a partner's perspective during a disagreement, or supporting a family member through hard times.

In the workplace, it could involve acknowledging a colleague's point of view during a team discussion, appreciating the challenges faced by your team, or leading with a focus on understanding rather than judgement. As empathetic communication becomes a habitual practice, we find our relationships deepening and our interactions becoming more rewarding.

2.6. Empathy: The Future of Communication

As we progress, society is increasingly recognizing empathy as a vital part of a comprehensive approach to communication. It encapsulates more than mere conveyance of messages - it shapes relationships, resolves conflicts, and fosters a better understanding of diverse viewpoints.

To thrive in an interconnected world, where communication cuts across various cultures and contexts, incorporating empathy into our communication strategies is the way forward. Ready to muster the power of empathy? Begin by understanding, practicing, and advocating for empathetic communication one step at a time.

After all, the journey towards a more compassionate world begins with a single empathetic conversation. We must remember, empathy, in all its profundity, begins when we choose to truly listen and understand each other, enriching our collective journey in this labyrinth of life.

Suit yourself with the power of empathy in the realm of communication, and witness the transformation it can bring in your everyday interactions, professional or personal alike. Empathy in action awaits you!

Chapter 3. Emotional Intelligence: The Foundation

In the realm of human interactions and communication, emotional intelligence forms the bedrock. The concept of emotional intelligence lies at the intersection of mind and heart, shaping the way we engage with ourselves and others. The influence of emotional intelligence extends from our personal relationships to our professional encounters. Our cognition, thoughts, feelings, and responses are guided by this subtle yet significant framework, and understanding it is vital to transforming the way we communicate.

3.1. The Essence of Emotional Intelligence

Emotional intelligence (EI), at its core, is the ability to understand and manage your own emotions along with those of others. This ability is divided into four primal components.

1. Self-awareness: The ability to accurately perceive your emotions in the moment and understand your tendencies across various situations.

2. Self-management: The application of awareness to staying flexible and directing your behavior positively.

3. Social Awareness: Understanding and picking up on others' emotions and understanding what is really going on.

4. Relationship Management: the capability to inspire, influence, and connect to others and manage conflict.

These components serve as a roadmap to navigate our emotional landscape and influence the way we translate these emotions in our daily communications.

3.2. Emotional Intelligence and Self

Jumping into the first component, self-awareness educates us about our internal states—understanding our strengths, weaknesses, needs, and drives. This element of emotional intelligence is essential to recognize the emotions that underlie our reactions and responses to different situations. Insight into our complex emotional states can aid in building an emotional vocabulary, providing us with the verbal precision needed to communicate accurately and effectively.

Next, we turn to self-management — a skill that regulates our emotions through self-control. Maintaining the balance of emotions is crucial in preventing impulsive or counterproductive reactions. In practising emotional self-regulation, we also nurture adaptability and resilience.

3.3. Emotional Intelligence and Others

The next pillar of emotional intelligence is social awareness. This facet involves empathy, organizational awareness, and-service orientation. Sharpening our perception of others' emotions helps us to understand multiple perspectives, fostering an environment rich in diversity. Recognizing and understanding these feelings can lead to more constructive communication, fostering healthier relationships.

Finally, the fourth segment, relationship management, imparts the ability to handle and inspire emotions in others in order to foster leadership, influence, change catalyst, conflict management, teamwork, and collaboration. Emotionally intelligent people can foster fulfilling relationships by managing their own emotions and handling others' emotions effectively.

3.4. Cultivating Emotional Intelligence

Now that the foundational components of emotional intelligence have been established, it becomes pivotal to understand its development. Unlike IQ, which remains somewhat constant throughout life, emotional intelligence can be nurtured and developed.

A few steps to increase your emotional intelligence are:

- Practice Reflective Listening: Listening is a keystone communication skill that involves not only hearing the spoken words but also understanding the emotions behind them.

- Develop Insight Through Mindfulness: Practicing mindfulness ushers us into the present moment, calibrating our focus on our own feelings and emotions and those of others around us.

- Maintain an Emotion Diary: Journaling activities, emotions, and responses help in gaining a lucid understanding of one's emotional blueprint.

- Seek feedback: Actively seek constructive feedback to get a clear perspective on your emotions and the impact they have on others.

Cultivating emotional intelligence does not happen overnight, it's a long-term commitment and a journey of self-discovery, connection, and transformation.

3.5. Emotional Intelligence in Communication

At the intersection of emotional intelligence and communication, lies the power to convey ideas in a manner that resonates with the emotions of others. Empathetic communication is composed of a balance of expressing ourselves authentically and responsibly, and listening with an intent to understand and validate.

EI guided communication aids in conflict resolutions, builds stronger relationships, and improves personal and professional relationships. It's about harnessing the power of emotion to enrich our connections, rather than letting them be a hindrance. A high level of emotional intelligence will aid in transforming linear, transactional interactions to dynamic, relational connections.

3.6. Conclusion

Emotional intelligence acts as a key for unlocking robust communication channels. Its grasp allows us to reap rich dividends not just in our personal relationships but also in our professional sphere. The connection between emotional intelligence and effective communication is a tapestry woven with the threads of empathy, compassion, understanding, and authentic expression. With the foundational knowledge of emotional intelligence in hand, we're equipped to start transforming not just our communication, but our relationships, our decisions, and our lives.

Remember, emotions don't hinder our rationality—they inform it. Emotional intelligence is not about subsiding emotions; it's about understanding them, managing them, and using them to enhance our lives and our interactions. The journey of emotional intelligence is as profound as it is transformative. And this journey begins with understanding its foundation.

Chapter 4. The Role of Empathy in Effective Communication

Understanding and expressing empathy is a fundamental part of human communication. It enables individuals to gather insights into other's feelings, thoughts, and experiences, fostering connection and promoting mutual understanding. This fundamental attribute plays a critical role in effective communication and has profound implications across personal and professional domains.

4.1. The Concept of Empathy

Empathy is the capacity to understand or feel what another person is experiencing, quite literally "walking in their shoes." It's about feeling and understanding a person's emotion as if it were your own. It's an unspoken form of communication—a visceral understanding that goes beyond words. Empathy evokes connotations of warmth, understanding, and compassion, and is crucial for harmonious human relationships.

There are primarily two types of empathy: cognitive and affective. Cognitive empathy relates to the ability to comprehend someone's perspective or mental state. It involves understanding another's feelings without necessarily sharing them. On the other hand, affective empathy is about sharing the emotional experience of others, often inciting sympathetic emotions like compassion. Both elements work synergistically to shape our responses to others' experiences.

4.2. Empathy and Communication

At its core, communication is about sharing and understanding meanings. Empathy enables the sender of a message to phrase their communication in a way that the receiver will understand and appreciate. Conversely, it allows the receiver to grasp the emotional context behind the sender's words. Thus, empathy enables a deeper harmony between the intellectual and emotional components of communication.

Empathy in the communication context means knowing the right words to say to someone who's in a specific emotional state and understanding when to say them. It's about being able to talk while taking into account how the other person will receive and interpret it. Furthermore, it involves recognizing when silence speaks louder than words and using non-verbal cues effectively.

4.3. Empathy in Personal Relationships

In family life and friendships, empathy plays a major role in strengthening bonds and resolving conflicts. When people genuinely express empathy towards each other's feelings, it builds trust, reduces anxiety, and fosters mutual respect. From parents' empathy towards their children's struggles to friends supporting each other in times of crisis, empathy allows for loving and understanding relationships.

Moreover, empathy encourages personal growth by promoting openness to diverse experience and viewpoints. By empathizing, people can appreciate various experiences and perspectives within their relationships, promoting personal growth and enriching their worldview.

4.4. Empathy in Professional Relationships

Empathy isn't limited to personal relationships—it's equally important in the professional arena. Empathetic leaders foster better team collaboration and higher employee morale, driving improved organizational success.

In conflict resolution and negotiation, understanding the concerns and viewpoints of all parties involved allows for tailored solutions that satisfy everyone's needs. By recognizing the underlying emotions and beliefs driving others' actions, one can communicate more effectively, leading to greater productivity, satisfaction, and engagement.

When employed in customer relations, the empathetic approach leads to better customer satisfaction rates, brand loyalty, and successful customer interactions. A simple act of mirroring a customer's emotions and genuinely understanding the problem can stand as a testament to the company's commitment to its customers.

4.5. Enhancing Empathy

While some individuals may naturally hold a higher empathetic ability, empathy is acquired and cultivated through experiences and conscious practice. Regularly practice active listening, give your complete attention to the speaker, and open yourself to their perspective. Note the emotions expressed in their words and respond with genuine understanding.

Training and workshops aiming to improve empathy often incorporate role-playing exercises. Role-playing encourages individuals to experience a situation from another's perspective, offering firsthand empathy-building opportunities. Similarly, consuming various forms of media that depict diverse life experiences can also help enhance empathetic understanding.

4.6. Conclusion

Embracing empathy in communication paves the way towards more sincere, effective, and enriching interactions. Regardless of the context, an empathetic approach can transform the way we comprehend each other, our world, and ourselves. As we explore the power of empathy, we prepare to enhance our relationships and influence our society positively. After all, human life thrives on the quality of its relationships, and those relationships are built on the strong foundation of empathy.

Chapter 5. Understanding and Managing Emotions: A Guide

One of the pivotal steps in mastering emotional intelligence is learning to understand and manage emotions. This is not about curtailing our emotions or restraining them; it is about recognizing them, making sense of them and utilizing this understanding to guide our actions and behaviors.

5.1. The Science Behind Emotions

Emotions aren't simply arbitrary feelings we experience sharply at times. They're grounded in a combination of psychology, neurology, and sociology, making them a complex aspect of human life. At the neurological level, an emotional response is the brain's way of reacting to stimuli in our environment, typically brought on by an external event.

In its most basic form, the process begins with the sensory organs — such as the eyes or ears — which pick up environmental cues and send these data to the brain. The brain, particularly the limbic system — a part of the brain associated with emotion, behavior, and memory — then processes this information. In response, it generates an emotional reaction, such as happiness, fear, anger, or sadness.

Likewise, our emotions also have a sociological aspect. Societies and cultures define the accepted ways to experience and express emotions. The social norms, sometimes referred to as "feeling rules," can influence how we express our emotions and how we interpret the emotions of others.

5.2. Identifying Emotions

Most people can identify extreme emotions such as joy when they win a lottery or sadness for the loss of a loved one. The trickier task comes with identifying subtle emotions, those slight shifts in our mood throughout the day that, if not recognized, can alter our emotional state drastically.

Emotional self-awareness, an essential facet of emotional intelligence, is the ability to identify and understand our emotions and their impact on our behavior. It allows us to perceive our emotional reactions to situations and understand the way those reactions affect our behaviors and decisions. Self-awareness helps us recognize when we are stressed, joyful, frustrated, or calm, and it provides a context for understanding not just our feelings, but also the behavior those feelings may cause.

To enhance emotional self-awareness, consider journaling about your feelings and reactions, noting any patterns or triggers. Practice mindfulness, focusing not just on tasks, but also on sensory experiences, thoughts, and emotions at any given moment.

5.3. Managing Your Emotions

Understanding your emotions is one thing, putting understanding into practice to better manage your emotions is another. Emotion management is not designed to suppress or discard emotions, but rather to acknowledge, understand, and effectively express them.

Self-management, another aspect of emotional intelligence, is the ability to regulate emotions, particularly the spontaneous response to situations, to enable us to think clearly and act appropriately. It's about transforming negative emotional reactions into positive outcomes.

To improve your self-management skills, begin by recognizing the difference between responding and reacting. Reacting is often an immediate, thoughtless action prompted by an emotion, whereas responding involves more cognitive processes – understanding the situation, considering the consequences of different actions, and selecting an appropriate action.

Use stress management techniques such as deep breathing and mindfulness exercises. Engage in activities that aid in expressing emotions like art, music, or physical activities. Practicing empathy, which is the understanding and sharing of other people's feelings, could also be a powerful tool in managing emotions.

5.4. Understanding Others' Emotions

The ability to understand others' emotions is vital for building successful relationships, both in personal and professional contexts. This relates to a concept known as empathy – the ability to understand, engage with and respond appropriately to the emotions of others.

Empathy enables us to build strong, supportive relationships, fosters collaboration, and reduces conflict. It plays a critical role in teams as it allows us to interpret unspoken emotions carried by nonverbal signals, improving overall communication.

To cultivate empathy, start by developing active listening skills. This involves fully focusing on the speaker, withholding judgment, reflecting, clarifying, summarizing, and sharing. It goes beyond being quiet while the other person is talking, and into engaging with the speaker and showing them you understand their feelings and perspectives.

In summary, understanding and managing emotions are critical components of emotional intelligence and key to enhancing our personal and professional relationships. It involves recognizing and acknowledging our emotions and those of others, and appropriately responding to them. Understanding and managing emotions isn't a destination but rather a lifelong journey, an ongoing process of growth requiring patience, practice, and commitment. The better we get at it, the more fruitful our communications and relationships will be.

Chapter 6. Bridging Gaps: Case Studies in Empathetic Communication

In a world where communicating effectively is paramount to our personal and professional achievements, a crucial, yet often overlooked ingredient, empathy, without doubt, has the power to bridge the gaps festering misunderstandings can form. Going beyond sympathy, empathy requires us to immerse ourselves in the viewpoint and emotions of others - an act that not only manifests understanding but sows the seeds of compassion and connection.

6.1. The Role of Empathy in Communication

Understanding how feelings, thoughts, and attitudes shape communication lies at the core of Emotional Intelligence. Concepts such as self-awareness, self-regulation, motivation, and social skills may be part of our everyday lexicon, but they all orbit around one essential central point: empathy.

Empathy forms the foundation of effective communication by allowing us to register how our words and actions resonate with others. It builds a bridge between sender and receiver, sharpening the message's accuracy and fostering a bond of common understanding. A perception of shared experience incites trust, breaks down barriers, and encourages open dialogue.

Two key types of empathy shape communication: cognitive empathy (understanding someone's point of view) and emotional empathy (sharing someone's feelings). A balanced combination of both lies at the heart of empathetic communication.

6.2. Empathy in Action: A Case Study on Customer Service

Let us now look at a pioneering example from the world of customer service, a field typically riddled with conflict and frustration. The Zappos call center, an e-commerce giant, stands as a beacon showcasing the transformative potential of empathy in every customer interaction.

At Zappos, representatives were trained not just to resolve issues but to connect with customers on a personal level. This groundbreaking approach involved abolishing scripts and time limits, giving employees more flexibility and the opportunity to lend an empathetic ear to customers. The results were astonishing: customer satisfaction escalated, return rates dropped, and the company's reputation received a significant boost.

6.3. Transforming Workplace Communication: The Google Case Study

In the realm of organizational communication, Google's "Project Aristotle" stands as a testament to the power of empathy in fostering team success. The project initially aimed to identify the magic formula for team effectiveness, expecting intricate strategies and complex algorithms to be the answer. However, the project's findings leaned heavily toward soft skills and emphatically underscored the role of empathy in team dynamics.

The key result from Project Aristotle was the discovery of 'psychological safety,' a term coined by Harvard Business School professor Amy Edmondson. Teams with high psychological safety are characterized by members feeling safe to take risks and be vulnerable in front of each other - a direct byproduct of empathy. Google discovered that this seemingly soft and intangible factor was critical to a team's performance and success.

6.4. Harnessing Empathy in Mediation: A Case Study

Migrating to a different domain, let's consider the role of empathy in conflict resolution, specifically in mediation. Here, we tap into the story of a mediator who, under the pseudonym "Ms. A," participated in a Harvard Negotiation Project.

At first, Ms. A struggled with tense and hostile conversations, unable to move parties toward resolution. However, when she shifted her approach from focusing solely on negotiation techniques to incorporating more empathy, she noticed a significant change. By showing understanding towards each party's perspectives and emotions, she was able to navigate the parties toward mutually satisfactory resolutions.

Each of the above case studies frames a different scene on the canvas of empathetic communication. Crossing sectors from customer service to corporate communication and conflict resolution, they underline empathy's timeless and universal potential.

6.5. Implementing Empathetic Communication: A Step-by-Step Guide

Implementing empathetic communication involves weaving in conscious and intentional steps into our everyday communication.

1. **Understand emotional language:** Start by becoming more

aware of emotional language and non-verbal cues. This helps attune you to the feelings and emotions of others.

2. **Practice active listening:** Make a conscientious effort to listen actively, giving the speaker your undivided attention.

3. **Show understanding:** Show empathy by reflecting what you've heard back to the communicator, signaling you recognize and understand their perspective.

4. **Suspend judgment:** Attempt to delay forming an opinion or judgment, creating a safer space for the communicator to express themselves.

5. **Demonstrate compassion:** Use reassuring language and positive body language to show that you care and understand.

Colonizing the abstract terrain of empathy may seem daunting, but it is not impossible. As we grow our empathy muscles, both personally and professionally, we unlock the potential to transform not just our communication but our entire relationship landscape. As our case studies demonstrate, the journey of empathy-centric communication opens up untold possibilities; the time to embark on it is now. The future isn't far when the ubiquitous motto for all forms of communication will likely be: "Empathize, connect, and thrive."

Chapter 7. Tools to Hone Your Emotional Intelligence

We begin our exploration by understanding the concept of emotional intelligence (EI) in depth. EI, a term coined by psychologists John D. Mayer and Peter Salovey, and popularized by psychologist and author Daniel Goleman, refers to the ability to identify, understand, and manage not just one's own emotions, but also the emotions of others. This capability equips an individual to navigate social complexities, make informed decisions, and forge stronger interpersonal relationships.

7.1. The Building Blocks of Emotional Intelligence

Understanding the following four key components of EI provides a foundation on which we can build our EI toolkit:

- Self-awareness: This is the ability to understand one's own emotions in real time. It involves acknowledging how our emotions shape our thoughts, influence our behavior, and impact others.

- Self-management: This quality refers to our capability in controlling our impulses and managing our emotional reactions to situations.

- Social awareness: This is characterized by the ability to understand and respond appropriately to the emotions of others, and contextually comprehend the dynamics of social interactions.

- Relationship management: Lastly, this refers to the ability to forge and sustain positive relationships, communicate effectively, and manage conflicts.

Understanding these building blocks is the first step in scrutinizing our emotional landscape.

7.2. Self-Assessment: The First Tool

The journey towards honing emotional intelligence begins with self-reflection and assessment of one's current emotional abilities. One effective method is undergoing a 360-degree feedback assessment. In this process, input is gathered from individuals across the respondent's professional and personal life, such as colleagues, managers, family, and friends. This allows for a comprehensive view of one's emotional competencies, strengths, and areas for improvement.

7.3. Developing Self-awareness

Meditation and mindfulness practices have long been associated with inducing a heightened sense of self-awareness. Regular mindfulness practices can train us to become more observant of our thoughts and feelings, making it possible to identify and label our emotions accurately. This can help curb habitual reactive patterns that might hinder effective communication.

7.4. Enhancing Self-Management

Maintaining an emotional journal is another effective tool for EI enhancement. By logging emotional experiences, their causes, and our responses to them, we can monitor our emotional triggers and develop strategies to manage them. This practice fosters self-control, adaptability, and resilience to stress.

7.5. Nurturing Social-Awareness

Active listening and observation are key facets of social awareness. Tools like non-verbal cues, body language, tone of voice, and actively seeking clarifications can aid in understanding others' perspectives, thereby preventing miscommunication and fostering empathy.

7.6. Achieving Skilled Relationship Management

The ultimate goal of honing EI is to foster stronger, more fulfilling relationships. A potent tool for this is assertive communication, which is characterized by expressing needs and feelings in an open, honest, and respectful manner. Regular practice of assertive communication can result in an increased capacity for conflict resolution, teamwork, and leadership.

7.7. Harnessing the Power of EI Tools

With familiarity and consistent practice of these tools, an individual can begin to see a transformation in their ability to interpret and control their emotional responses, as well as understand and respond to the emotions of others. This increased aptitude for emotional intelligence will lead to more meaningful connections, meaningful exchanges, and overall success in personal and professional relationships.

7.8. EI: A Lifelong Journey

Remember that improving emotional intelligence is not a one-and-done endeavor. Various stages of life will necessitate different emotional skills, and challenges will test your emotional strengths regularly. Stay committed to self-improvement and empathetic communication, continue learning, and constantly revisit and adapt your EI toolkit. This journey towards higher emotional intelligence is a lifelong and rewarding pursuit.

In conclusion, emotional intelligence is an indispensable skill in the contemporary world. Its significance cannot be understated for improving interpersonal relationships, enhancing communication, and promoting personal development. Building and honing your EI can reshape not just your personal and professional relationships, but also your worldview, helping you connect on a more profound level with the emotions and experiences of others. Remember, the journey to emotional intelligence starts with you!

Chapter 8. Creating Empathetic Cultures in Organizations

In the wake of a rapidly evolving global business environment, it has become paramount for organizations to employ tactics that strategically promote empathetic cultures. Empathy is not just a need in personal relationships, but extends equally in fostering the professional ones, grounding them in a shared understanding and mutual respect.

8.1. The Quintessence of Empathy

Empathy is the ability to understand and share the feelings of others, and in the context of an organization, it means creating a nurturing environment where employees feel heard, understood, and valued. It extends far beyond just understanding the sentiments of others - it involves active listening, validation, and reciprocation.

The purpose of empathy within the organization is two-fold: firstly, it paves the way to a healthier workplace environment, and secondly, it ensures that the employees better understand their clients' needs and expectations, thereby enhancing customer loyalty.

8.2. Building Empathetic Cultures: The Journey

Creating an empathetic culture requires a shared vision and commitment at all levels within the organization. This journey starts not at the grassroots, but at the leadership level.

A fundamental change in leadership's mindset considered empathy as a sign of weakness, is today hailed as a testament to great leadership. Leaders who are empathetic foster a culture of open communication, and appreciation. They lead by example, donating their time and energy to understand their teams, valuing their input, thereby showing their worth, and earning their respect.

8.3. The Role of Emotional Intelligence

Emotional intelligence (EQ) is the cornerstone of creating empathetic cultures. High EQ leaders are equipped with the ability to recognize, understand, and manage both their own emotions and those of their employees. Encouraging leaders to attend EQ development workshops can help foster the growth of emotional intelligence in an organization.

Improving EQ within the organization centers on five key domains: self-awareness, self-regulation, motivation, empathy, and social skills. Balancing these domains enables employees to communicate better, alleviate stress, overcome challenging situations, and collaborate efficiently.

8.4. Creating the Necessary Systems

Creating an empathetic culture doesn't happen spontaneously; it requires strategic planning and implementation. An Empathy Development Plan (EDP) provides a framework for the instillation of empathy within each team, each department, and ultimately, the entire organization.

A comprehensive EDP should include detailed strategies, monitoring mechanisms, and key periods of review to assess progress. It necessitates employee engagement programs that focus on empathy, empathetic leadership training sessions, and tools for assessing the culture's empathy quotient.

8.5. The Empathy Feedback System

Receiving and giving feedback empathetically can transform the dynamics of the workplace. It leads to a more constructive approach to critique and counters the dread associated with performance assessments. Incorporating empathetic feedback, leaders can instate a constructive dialogue, promoting a mindset of growth rather than fear.

The feedback system should encourage active listening, understanding, non-judgmental stance and articulating thoughts and feelings; it's not just about providing feedback but ensuring the feedback is received well. Employee feedback should also be given due importance, as empathy is bidirectional.

8.6. Empathy and Diversity: Hand in Hand

Promoting empathy in the workplace is essential for addressing and appreciating diversity. Respect for different perspectives enhances team collaboration, fosters new ideas, and creates an inclusive environment where everyone feels a sense of belonging.

To effectively foster empathy amidst diversity, organizations should focus on unbiased hiring practices, empowering diverse voices, promoting respect and understanding, and educating employees about different cultures and viewpoints.

8.7. The Long-term Impact

Empathetic cultures have far-reaching effects on the employee experiences, client satisfaction, and bottom-line business outcomes.

They foster environments of mutual respect and understanding, encouraging ideas and innovation, and ultimately, driving growth. The organizations instilled with empathy are better equipped to navigate the ever-changing business landscape and stand a better chance of emerging victorious even during the hardest of times.

Creating empathetic cultures requires mindfulness, dedication, and strategic planning, but the outcome is worth every ounce of effort - organizations become not just profitable, but an institute where individuals grow, thrive and become the best versions of themselves.

Chapter 9. The Future of Communication: The Empathy Shift

"Changes are coming," they say. Technology continues to advance at an astonishing rate, and with it, the ways in which we communicate are ever-evolving. Yet, one aspect of human interaction remains instrumental yet under-explored: empathy. In moulding the future of communication, we are standing at a critical juncture, a juncture where the importance of empathy is unequivocally resurging.

9.1. The Mainstreaming of Empathy

Where did this come from? The 'empathy shift' can be traced back to the proliferation of digital technologies augmenting human connections. Globally, individuals are gaining ease in sharing their voices and emotions on public platforms. As a consequence, the need for empathy in our listening and speaking is heightened like never before.

Whereas yesteryear's cultural composition was largely homogenous, today's society pulsates with a myriad of different cultures, ideologies, and belief systems. Empathy in communication has transitioned from being a soft skill to an essential skill. It's no longer just about understanding what is being said, but understanding the emotional churn that propelled those words. It's not just decoding a message but also navigating the emotional landscape that surrounds it.

9.2. The Shift: What Does It Mean?

While empathy in communication is not a novel concept, the

aforementioned 'empathy shift' is unique in marking a broadening of our awareness of emotions. This shift signifies a transition from cognitive to empathetic communication — where we understand 'how' and 'why' a message is being communicated, as much as 'what' is being communicated.

When we think of empathy in communication, it's not just the avoidance of misunderstandings. It's about getting to the soul of what a person is saying — the fears, hopes, and aspirations that their words are woven around. It's about respecting their narratives and honouring their emotional narrative. This approach gifts us the opportunity to create a network of trust based on mutual respect and understanding.

9.3. Incorporating Empathy in Various Forms of Communication

What does this shift look like in practical terms? To find out, let's explore the ways empathy can be incorporated into different forms of communication.

In face-to-face communication, showing empathy means active listening, mirroring non-verbal cues, and reflecting feelings back. Physical expressions of empathy, such as a hand on the shoulder or a reassuring smile, play an equally crucial part.

When it comes to non-verbal communication, read the room — take note of body language, facial expressions, and tone of voice. Remember, empathy in communication transcends spoken words. Noting these subtle cues can open a gateway for a more profound understanding and connection.

In written communication, it's about crafting our message considering the reader's context, emotions, and potential interpretations. This approach enables a holistic and thoughtful message that radiates understanding.

However, with the rise of digital communication, empathy takes on a new imperative. The lack of physical presence and limited non-verbal cues can easily cause misinterpretation. This calls for a different approach, one centered around extending emotional understanding even in the absence of physical presence.

In video calls, even if the internet lags, let the empathy flow smoothly. Pay heed to digital body language, such as response timings, punctuation, and the use of emoticons. More importantly, foster a culture that promotes emotional well-being and ensures everyone feels heard.

9.4. A Culture of Empathetic Communication

Creating such a culture requires a deliberate effort. But, if you're keen on fostering an environment of empathy, the first step is to build a culture that encourages vulnerability.

Empathy necessitates the courage to be in touch with one's own feelings and the willingness to share them. It requires acknowledging emotions instead of dismissing or overriding them. Fostering an environment that values vulnerability makes room for empathy, paving the way for more profound connections and effective communication.

9.5. Empathy-Driven Leadership

For organizations, embedding empathy in communication might seem challenging; but it is achievable. It starts with leadership. When leaders walk the talk, employees follow suit. Leaders who listen empathetically, consider different perspectives, and value emotions can foster a more inclusive and productive work environment.

9.6. The Empathetic Future

The future of communication lies in strengthening emotional connections — something that rigid structures and traditional management styles have often overlooked. Bracing for this shift requires embracing empathy and making it the linchpin of our communication style.

As we step into this future, we step into a world where empathy is valued over efficiency, emotional intelligence over rigid hierarchy, and individual well-being over systematic rigidity.

In a world marred by increasing complexities, fostering communication marked by empathy is not just an investment but a necessity. It promulgates hope, ushers in change, and leads us towards a more empathetic, understanding world — a world where we are truly connected and authentically understood.

Remember, the future is not something that happens to us, it's something we create. So, let's build a future where the empathy shift is not just an anomaly but the norm in how we communicate, connect, and thrive!

Chapter 10. From Theory to Practice: Implementing Emotional Intelligence

While emotional intelligence was encapsulated in a tidy theoretical framework by pioneers like Daniel Goleman, the challenge lies in translating these theories into real-world practice. Our focus in this segment is to help you navigate this gently, yet purposefully.

10.1. Understanding Emotional Intelligence

Emotional Intelligence, often expressed via the acronym EI, is the ability to manage our own emotions and that of others. It's also to perceive, evaluate, and control emotions, making for more effective communication and person-to-person relationships. In essence, it forms the core of our interactions and deeply impacts our professional life, personal relationships, and our relationship with ourselves.

10.2. The Components of Emotional Intelligence

Emotional intelligence comprises five key components as outlined by Goleman: self-awareness, self-regulation, motivation, empathy, and social skills.

1. Self-Awareness: This refers to understanding your own emotions, strengths,weaknesses, and gauging how they affect your thoughts and behavior.

2. Self-Regulation: This involves managing your emotions in healthy ways, taking responsibility for your actions, and behaving in a socially acceptable manner.

3. Motivation: It refers to the drive to achieve for the sake of achievement.

4. Empathy: This represents understanding and sharing the feelings of others.

5. Social Skills: These are skills required to build and nurture relationships, manage conflict, inspire and influence others.

10.3. Integrating Emotional Intelligence into Daily Life

On a practical level, integrating Emotional Intelligence might seem daunting. One must remember is that it's not a destination, but instead, a journey of understanding and awareness. Below are methods and tools to help you implement emotional intelligence.

1. **Start with Self-awareness**: Begin your day with a moment of self-reflection. Take some time to identify your emotions and feelings, and how they might be affecting your actions.

2. **Practice Mindfulness**: Mindfulness involves being fully engaged in the present moment. It allows for increased self-awareness and a greater understanding of your emotions and reactions.

3. **Journaling**: Taking a few minutes every day to note your feelings, emotions, reactions, and thoughts can be valuable. It helps to identify patterns, triggers and also brings into focus areas you may need to work on.

4. **Active Listening**: This is not just about hearing the words being said but understanding the complete message being delivered. One of the ways to improve relationships and understand the emotions of others more deeply.

5. **Empathy Practice**: Actively pay attention to the feelings of people around you, try to understand their perspective. Empathy leads to better interpersonal relationships.

10.4. Emotional Intelligence in the Workplace

The business world has been astoundingly perceptive of Emotional Intelligence because it leads to a healthier workplace culture fostering better collaboration and increasing productivity.

1. **Leadership and Emotional Intelligence**: Good leaders frequently exhibit high emotional intelligence. They are capable of recognising and understanding their team members' emotions, enabling better decision making and conflict resolution, whilst promoting a positive team culture.

2. **EI and Communication**: With emotional intelligence, communication becomes more effective and empathetic. It allows for understanding the emotional state of the person you're communicating with, leading to a better response and engagement.

3. **Career Advancement**: Careers and indeed organizations can thrive when emotional intelligence is prioritised. Being able to manage emotions can help tackle stress effectively, take criticism constructively, and collaborate with others, all key factors in career progression.

10.5. Conclusion

While it's a journey to fully integrate emotional intelligence into our lives, its deepest value is in the transformation it brings about. Emotional Intelligence is much more than a buzzword, it's a unique toolset. Implementing Emotional Intelligence could, perhaps more accurately, be termed as one of those profound shifts in human consciousness that occur when we start really seeing others - and truly observing ourselves. Only then do communication and relationships truly find their fullest expression.

The practical application of emotional intelligence fosters a harmony between the mind and heart, facilitating a concert of empathetic exchange and improving our personal and professional communication landscape. Are you ready to harness the transformative power of Emotional Intelligence? Your journey begins now, and every step forward counts.

Chapter 11. The Transformative Power of Empathy: A Summary

Understanding empathy and its transformative power is essential not just in the personal domain but carries significant weight in professional areas. Let's dive deeper and explore the various facets of empathy and its impact.

11.1. Empathy: The Basic Understanding

Empathy, defined as the ability to understand and share the feelings of others, is rooted in our human social fabric. It is a bridge that not only helps us connect but also forms the foundation for meaningful interactions. It is an essential trait in the listener, allowing for the possible understanding and replication of the emotional state of the speaker. It allows for an emotional resonance that deepens our interpersonal relationships.

11.2. The Dimensions of Empathy

Empathy is composed of two primary dimensions: cognitive empathy and emotional (or affective) empathy. Cognitive empathy implies understanding the perspective and the mental state of another person, whereas emotional empathy refers to sharing and resonating with someone else's emotional experiences.

Cognitive empathy enables the receiver to grasp the thoughts and feelings of the speaker without necessarily experiencing the emotions. It involves perspective-taking, in essence, allowing us to "step into another person's shoes".

On the other hand, emotional empathy allows us to share the feeling states with the speaker. It requires a strong emotional bond and the capacity to perceive and be moved by the other person's emotions. Emotional empathy is deeply personal and involves not only understanding but sharing another person's emotional experience.

11.3. Empathy in Professional Communication

Studies reveal that empathy plays a significant role in professional communication. It allows for a better understanding of colleagues, clients, stakeholders, and aids in delivering precisely what is desired. Not only does empathy improve communication, but it also enhances collaboration and teamwork.

Empathy can help build more robust and productive relationships by reducing conflicts and building a bond based on mutual understanding. In leadership and management, empathy is considered a crucial skill. A leader who can understand and empathize with his team members can motivate and get the best out of them.

11.4. Empathy in Personal Relationships

Empathy has transformative power in personal relationships. It helps individuals to understand their partners, friends, or family members better, leading to stronger, more fulfilling connections. Empathy allows for deeper connections by encouraging understanding and sharing of experiences.

When we empathize with our friends or family members, we can understand their viewpoints better and avoid making assumptions. Empathy can help reduce arguments and conflicts, and promote harmony in relationships.

11.5. Empathy and Emotional Intelligence

Empathy is a critical aspect of emotional intelligence. Emotional intelligence, defined as the capacity to be aware of, control, and express our emotions, and handle interpersonal relationships judiciously and empathetically, is key to cultivating empathy.

Our emotional intelligence allows us to recognize and understand our own emotions and the emotions of others. It includes perceiving the emotional undercurrent of the situation, using emotions to facilitate thinking, understanding emotional meanings, and managing our own and others' emotions.

Cultivating empathy as part of emotional intelligence allows us to improve our understanding of others and deepen our connections with them.

11.6. Empathy: A Learned Skill

While it may appear that empathy might be an innate human tendency, research indicates that empathy can also be learned and strengthened through practice. With conscious effort and practice, individuals can improve their ability to empathize with others.

Balancing cognitive and emotional empathy is an important part of honing this skill. This balance allows us to understand another person's perspective and share their emotions without losing ourselves in the process.

11.7. Empathy to Empathetic Responding

Beyond empathetic understanding, empathetic responding is the step towards action. It is all about how we respond based on empathetic understanding. Empathetic responding involves not just understanding of the other person's emotions, but acting in a way that conveys that understanding.

Empathetic responding can be as simple as validating the other person's experience or offering words of comfort. It is a demonstration of our commitment to valuing the thoughts and feelings of others.

11.8. Transforming Empathy into Action

The transformation of empathy into action is what gives it true power. In professional or personal relationships, empathetic actions are those that not only indicate understanding but also showcase comfort, assistance, or rectification depending on the situation.

Turning empathy into action requires intentionality. It means actively listening to understand the other person's perspective, validating their emotions, and then offering a response that effectively communicates respect and understanding.

11.9. Conclusion

Embracing empathy reshapes our relationships and our communication patterns. Empathy can improve the quality of professional relationships, enhance personal connections, and pave the way for a more emotionally intelligent society. By recognizing its transformative power, we can better understand the experiences and emotions of those around us, granting us the ability to communicate more effectively and sincerely.

The transformative power of empathy is immense, as it is not just about understanding or sharing emotions, but about using this understanding to bring about deliberate actions. An empathic stance enables inherent respect, recognition and concern for others' experiences and emotions, leading to mutually beneficial interactions based on understanding and authenticity. The transformative power of empathy lays the foundation for emotionally intelligent communication - communication that resonates, communicates respect, considers perspectives and ultimately, builds connections.